FRAGMENTS OF DESIRE

The fifth selection of fourteen poems by the finest poetical voice of the post-war generation of English poets. Including the dramatic poem, Shadows and Realities.

"It is the gift of a special writer to be able to convey in words what she has seen and felt herself so that her readers see and feel what she has seen and felt."
Elizabeth Harvey (literary critic)

Shänne Sands

Further selections of poems by Shänne Sands

Vol.1   Fidelity Is For Swans
Vol.2   The Silver Hooves
Vol.3   Moonlight On Words
Vol.4   Night Song

FRAGMENTS OF DESIRE

Selected Poems By
SHÄNNE SANDS
Volume 5

www.footsteps.co

© Shänne Sands 2012

The right of Shänne Sands to be identified as the author of this work and illustrations has been asserted in accordance with sections 77 and 78 of the copyright designs and patents act 1988.

Fragments Of Desire

Footsteps Press first edition
www.footsteps.co

Cover design by Kevin Reilly and
Jackie Pascoe

Typeset by Jackie Pascoe

Set in century
ISBN 978-0-9566349-6-2

Reproduction of any or all of this work in any form, electronic or otherwise, is expressly forbidden without the prior contractual agreement of the author. Incidental illustrations are taken from the original hand written volumes by Shänne Sands.

This book is for those
whose minds are sealed
with words and
there remain

Poetry is life's wine

Incidental illustrations from the original hand written scripts

Poems

Shadows And Realities, (A Dramatic Poem)	1
On Reading Ben Johnson	16
Janna's Suitcase (An Epitaph)	17
You Are My Oasis	18
Revolve The Spinning Top	19
Poem Of Actuality	22
Wasted Time	24
Sunflowers	25
For My Poor Sick Brother Allan Edwin	26
Poet Follow Your Sadness	27
Eagles	28
Siste Viator	29
November Winds	30
On The Steps Of Morning	32

Shadows and Realities
A dramatic poem

Chorus

I am here to ask no questions of you all;
Tell you no lies -
But just to bring the Shadows
Into the light and let them speak.
I shall retreat gently without fuss
And let you watch the Shadows
Come alive.

Child

Mummy, mummy my doll is cracked her
Face is cracked and broken down one side.
And they said she was unbreakable.
My sweetest Amanda. My little doll
All broken and cracked down one side -

Mother

Now stop crying there's a good girl,
We'll take her to the doll's hospital
And they will make her well.
Everything breaks you know that and
Sometimes things become more
Precious when they're cracked -
Now stop crying come here and let me
Tidy your plaits!

Child

My sweetest Amanda will never be the same;
And I am lonely with my tidy hair.
Oh grown-ups don't understand that I hate tidy hair -
My father is so tidy and speaks such
A lot and Amanda is the only friend I've got.
Why did my doll break?
Why is my father so tidy?

Chorus

Mother and child a pretty scene --
The child is lonely and will soon
Grow up and stop calling for her
Mother who didn't understand anyway -
From womb to child the distance is
A long, long way and broken toys
And too much tidiness leaves only

A bridge of regrets and the last
Ribbon from the child's hair - before
Womanhood takes even that!

Father

How did the doll break?
We should send it back to the
Makers and get a new face.
They charged enough for the damned thing
Can't have the child crying all over
The place - If there's one thing
I can't stand that's a crying child -
Get the doll repaired for God's sake!

Mother

Yes, dear I'll see it's done, but she's
Asleep now and the house is quiet -
Come and have dinner and try this
Sherry it's dry and cold and full of grapes.
Let's talk - what did the papers say?
Someone came in for coffee and
The daily-help threw the news away!

Child

They think I'm asleep,
But I'm awake,
And all the curtains have come alive with faces.
My poor Amanda's face.
Mummy seemed to feel sorry, but
Daddy only thought of money and if I was asleep.
I really don't like daddy anymore -
I think he's what grown-ups call a bore.
I'd better say my prayers -
God-bless Amanda and make well -
God-bless my grannie for she is old -
God-bless Mummy and Daddy (but I don't mean it!)

Lover

Dearest, when I feel your body next
To mine I want to push life into you -
Fill your breast with milk made
From my kisses and see your belly
Swell, grow heavy with my child -

Mistress

I thought once how much your
Child would rejoice that we had
Made its life from all our passion -
And fashioned it with wine and verse -
But I was wrong.
Infants are cruel you know -
Selfish and cruel -
Now let me go -
I cannot bulge my belly with your child -
And give my womb's shelter
To a seed that will breed hate
From all our love -
And dis-like our sacred creed.

Lover

Sweetheart you are wrong -
Children are made for laughter and song
Part of you and part of me -
Better than both of us -
Let me empty myself into your womb
And our child will live
To see next year's spring.

Chorus

The Shadows of existence sing
And sway into the light of day -
Mothers and fathers treat the child with doubt -
The child's indifference is sadly true -
The lovers argue and then
Fall back into bed again -

Old Lady

I had children once and a husband
Who lingered in pubs and smelled of beer -
My son grew up and fled into
Some woman's bed then to
Australia I think -
My daughters gave themselves
Away to callers at the door -
One of them left a note -
'I'm getting married, mum,' she wrote -
A grandchild or two came after that -
And I heard something about a flat -

But I am old now and sit and think
Of the days that brought me here -
To the budgie in its cage
And the W.V.S. Friday call
But really I don't care at all!

Old Man

Oh, yes I drank and whored -
Even had a wife, but the bones
Grow thin and brittle and the
Air feels cold the day you
Suddenly grow old!
Memories of passion float across
The floor without faces -
Faces have no part in an old man's memory.

A Nun

I entered the convent door
When I was sixteen -
Mary Mother of God held my hand -
As years turned into vows I had to take -
Married to the Cross I walk
The convent floors and say my beads -
My head is always bent
And somewhere in my brain -
The torment of the prayers
Says I'm insane -

The Road Sweeper

Autumn leaves are the worst things
In the dirty streets -
They pile around the broom and get
In-between my feet -
Snow is filthy stuff all slush and ice,
But sweeping up souls is very nice -
People drop them everywhere
And wonder why I kick along
The leaves and cackle to myself
The lonely road sweeper on
The local thoroughfare!

Doctor

I treat the sick
All round the clock -

Have known some of them for years.
Break the news of birth and death
And then go home to rest.
Drugs and needles follow everywhere
And pain is like the rain it comes again and again.
Nights are filled with aches as patients
Take the pills that I prescribe -
My work is never done and I should
Like to go abroad,
But even there someone is bound to shout-
"Is there a doctor in the villa?"

A Prostitute

Hundreds of men have crawled
Up and down my legs -
Whipped my flesh with lashes
That cut and tore -
I felt nothing -
Only the money slung into the
Drawer and the pile of new
Sweaters lying in a heap mean
Anything to me -
Purity! What a joke!
I'm paid to stay this way -
And from my open door-way pick
Them up and lust them out of view -
I'm sure I've met you,
But you turn your head away -
Only I can afford to be honest
In the light of day!

Judge

The courts are silent -
The case is heard and the last
Strand of dust has been shaken
From my wig -
Is it for me to forgive the thief?
I can only give years away -
Other men's years -
To toil with locks and keys
And feel justice has been done -
There are nights when voices
Bang against my head -
And I toss and twist in bed -
And think seven years is a

Long, long time to spend
Behind a wall -
But mostly I rarely think -
And sentiment and law
Will always brawl!

Beauty

Let me at least stay free -
To embroider the days with gladness.
Let me at least hold hands over winding lanes;
That bring sunsets nearer to the grass.
For a while let something lovely
Bind the weather with gold leaves -
And gentle breezes shake the buds and flowers.
Hours come and go
With all kinds of drifting sand -
Let me cast my image on the
Stones and leave my message
By the trees for you to understand -

Chorus

Let them become Shadows again -
And leave the pain lying on the stage -
Maybe somewhere in Futurity
Hands will not wrinkle
And eyes not weep -
And the broken doll not close
Her eyes to sleep -
Lover to lover will gather sperm
To fill the womb with laughter -
The Shadows ask no questions -
Tell no lies -
Only serve the minute with
A thought that somewhere
We are all caught -
And bound to conditions
We have never thought enough about!
And standing on the edge of destiny
We raise a pathetic shout -
And pray on knees in bad repair -
Humanity is so unsure - so bleak -
That I'm now unable to speak -
Let them all dance and fade away -
And you go home
And leave this play.

Chorus Of Realities

We are the Realities -
We grip your waists -
With our amazing strength -
Until you perish from too
Much living confusion -
Mixing all Earth's illusion
Around our enormous Truth -
Which you never quite understand,
And uselessly deny -
Until circumstances irk
The reason from the sky
And bend you down -

Loneliness

Poets know me by another name -
Yet I am the same to most of you -
I do not fumble 'round your feet
For space to breathe -
I rise higher than you can ever be -
Tremendous in my reality -
I twist the heart and hurt the seeing eyes -
And dance a jig of circles near the wise -
Who pretend I am not there!
This is no vague feeling that I bring -
I am loneliness
Greater than a king -
My throne is made of
Longing's crimson-iron -
And tears are stitched
Into all the gowns I wear -
My crown is almost like a fire -
That blisters souls, where people used to be -
I am free to invade your most secret thoughts:
Plague you with all desperation's wit.
You cannot catch me as I flit
In one continuous, leaping, hurtful grind-
Into the aching core
Of all mankind -

Pain

I furrow through your bones
To puncture tiny holes of illness -
I am the burning needle in your groins
I open the body's honey-comb

And suck it dry -
My expansion in the heart
Causes you all to depart -
Since that is the reason
That you came, then you must
Enjoy my name -
I cut a passage through your grief -
And in the end I bring relief!

Despair

There is no dramatic entrance
I can make -
I arrived for my own sake -
Because I wanted to be here -
To watch the others -
They come and go along the flow of Time
Piercing the cunning games
With well-devised plots.
They cannot fool me who came
The day Eve stroked the serpent's head
Then fled to Adam's side
And with a long dreadful scream
Called my name out for the first time!
I came forward into existence
And now look back a long, long way -
And although I'm tired
I'm glad I came today -
To watch the others

Delight

I rarely come,
Not because I want to stay away,
My lamp shines for everyone
But you've pushed me as far away as you can.
Allowing me only moments of attendance.
You do not encourage
My kind of nourishment -
I am rather stronger than
The rest and although
You like me best you all
Stoop to clog yourselves
With beams from vile, unhealthy
Stars that shine into your Destinies
A weak compulsion -
'Till your throats shout for me to dance.

But long ago you let me down -
Now I rarely come -
My commands resist your kind of order -
For I dance only on
The border of your dreams.
And fade into oblivion with speed -
Leaving my resplendent touch
Behind to haunt you all -
As a thousand voices
Every thousand half seconds
Call and call -

Fear

What can I say for myself
That you do not know too well -
How many times have you felt
My chilled fingers on your backs?
You who have made bombs
Instead of songs
And dark murksome torture
Through the nights
Of all your generations -
What can I tell you
That you have not seen;
In the camps for you staged
Great plays for me to clap
My whips to and produce
My special horror look -
You have denied me nothing -
I cannot protest about such things
As neglect -
You have treated me so well.
That now I do not have to work alone,
But have great marshals to bear me along -
You lie at night wondering when
I'll strike and the enigma
That I whisper to the flies is this ...
No - I shall not tell you -
I have changed my mind -
For then you might not care
About me anymore -
My hour would lose its race
Against your sin -
So I'll strut and follow you about the house,
The streets, the wider roads of travel
Till you give in

And become my little lap dogs -
Shallow, timid and afraid -
O hollow cowards
All I respect is courage -
But heaven forgot to create
This special god!

Love

Do I dare speak?
How shall I begin?
Soaring from some great height
An exalted flight -
Sweeping you off your feet
As I usually do.
Or shall I begin softly
With tenderness, on tiptoe
With my head covered in white silk -
Shall I come tall as an Alpine day
With huge mountains blocking
My way to your heart -
Or shall I be small
And perfectly untouchable
In my beauty -
Or shall I stumble,
Lurch into mistakes and fright -
Leaving you to weep
Such sad weepings -
Shall I be buoyant
And float into you
Like an ocean would -
Filling your being with enough
Power to surmount every problem
Trying to force me out -
Or shall I not come at all -
And leave you free to cast yourselves
Into the seas of circumstance,
Where you will sink
And never know about me -
Would that be fair?
For although I do not offer fidelity
Only a promise of a kiss -
You should not miss my lottery tickets
Five for two-shillings on a hot day
For you might win.
I have always been a gamble -
But you might win!

Success

You know how I love to talk
About myself -
My ego is ulcer-ridden,
But I have organised my
Conversation to suit my moods -
I've worked for years to get
Where I am -
Many caught my kick on the way up!
I live now in the twilight of
Half-truth daring to tell no-one
Too much in-case I lose my mystery
And become like everyone else -
I am ruthless -
Well, you know that's how one must be -
Nothing must stand in my way -
I have no compassion
For king or beggar -
I put puppies out in the coldest rain -
And watch tears fall down
Lovely cheeks without wiping
One away -
I am skin deep -
I last only for today -
If I stop for one, brief moment
And take a rest,
They will forget my quest
And my ego will become obsolete -
So I must rush, must haste,
Must pack my case and flee -
Towards the winds that beckon me -
But I see a threatening, impending doom -
Standing silent in my room -
And I struggle with my laces
To make my get-away -
Without looking back -
I hurry, hurry to any convenient station
To catch the eternal train
Back to where I started from -
There was the same doom -
And the train had gone!

Sorrow

On bended knees I gave Time my pledge
To bind you to the dust's
Haziness behind the hedge of human crusts -

There can be no sparkling gems, where I fall -
Only tattered dress hems swinging
In a dark hall -
From the tops of desolate frames
Twisted with oppressed desire -
Caught between a cherished name
And the wounded liar -
If I cripple, bruise, molest the soul
Try to forgive -
I did not choose this noxious hour
Time made it live.

Chorus

I told you to go home
And leave the play -
To let the Shadows sway back
To where they came from -
But you did not listen.
From the very first day
You refused to obey -
Now you must remain right to the end
And that will be a task my friends -
For the Realities are not easy masters -
All I can offer to relieve
The tension is dear old Laughter
Who no-one can depress.

Laughter

How strange that I should suddenly feel sad!

Chorus Of Memories

There are too many of us
To speak all at once -
But it's difficult to restrain
Our torrent -
Our force, we do not tranquillise
Or try to appease -
We fit no passive cloaks
Upon the shoulders born to carry us.
Poignant for a foam-like second
Then acute with visions
Of yesterday's sunrise.
Dormant, tame, then smouldering
To all our waking fruitfulness -

Truth

When most denied, most alive -
When a castaway on overheated shores,
Or left standing in an empty field -
Where something more than peace
Heals the damage or crime -
When squeezed into overcrowded
Streets or left to freeze -
Or broken like tiny frail twigs
From young bushes -
Or like the palest wild rose -
Just daring to be fragrant -
Most holy, most sacred, most divine;
Neglected, but a giant against
The throng's pale insincerity -
There is only one shrine
Where miracles change
Water into wine -
And that O torn deceivers -
Is mine -

Hate

The raver's God am I -
Bearing the mob's lie -
On my ramble
Through the tangle
Of staring fools
Whose only tools
Are my mania for victims -
They pander to my whims
As dullards do -
And when I'm through
With them,
I break their stem
Of reason and run like mad -
I've always been a cad!

Hope And Faith

Perhaps we are the great deceivers
As we eternally promise -
Always together as we are
Afraid to be alone -
We roam the complete circle
Of all chance -
And secretly dance the strangled emotions

Into valleys they cannot escape from -
Being together we chat a lot -
And forget we're meant to be
Part of the patterns
Of reality -
And so we rarely happen -
When we remember - if we ever do -
It's almost like tiny transparent
Pearls of dew,
There only for the moment -
Before harsh downpours of rain
Breaks us up into fragments -
And we are scattered across
The everlasting shell
That holds the embryo of all things
Inside itself -

Chorus Of Realities

We are the Realities -
We come and go -
Go and come -
Beating an everlasting drum -
Banging out a rhythmic plea
For Shadows and Reality.

On Reading Ben Johnson

I have loved faces silvered with gloom
Faces dipped into light stolen from the moon -
I have loved faces humoured by the sun
Flickered by sunbeams as the day has run.

I have loved backs like perfect trees
Straight and firmed to thighs and knees
And hands where fingers like flowers
Sway away unpleasant hours -

I have loved eyes that shelter tears
Before they fall as fall the years
And merry eyes full of happy laughter
Eyes that sorrow cannot master -

I have loved voices that only echo right
I have loved voices heard in darkest night
Voices not deformed by angry lives
Voices free from vulgar thought or bribes.

I have loved lips that moulded rhyme -
Kissed the poets' words from every time -
Even if furious demons invent my pain
I shall love all these again -

Janna's Suitcase (An Epitaph)

A pink nightgown -
To fit a small five-year old -
A toothbrush also small
For a child to hold.
Her slippers soft and sweet,
Her dressing gown, which touches tiny feet.
Two day-dresses, which her mamma made.
Her white vests and knickers
With new socks and shoes.
Carefully laid within the suitcase;
Before it was locked
Janna could choose
A baby-doll, a rag-book, a wooden-toy.
A holiday, a journey, she waited
With such joy -
Her mother drew the curtains -
So Janna did not see
Outside a waiting wagon -
To ride the Jews away -
Into the mouth of a
    Monster dragon -

You Are My Oasis

You are my oasis
The fertile spot
In the desert of
My life -

From you and only you
Words will flow like water
From the underground-well -
The spiritual oath
Needed by poets
Will always be sacred -

You are my illustration -
More than my ideal -
My symbol of victory
Like the leaf of a palm-tree -
But you are also my pannier -
A kind of beast of burden
Carrying all the mistakes
I must never make -

And in the end as in the beginning
You are my love -
Where all poetry
Becomes leopards
Wild, untamed and free -

Where panic ends in sleep -
And muddy years have moved away -
No rust will settle on your panoply -
No brittle speech
Will rot your poems
Or mine -

You are my open respect
For bits of typewriters
And pieces of white paper -
Although the pain is
Terrible at times -
You are my altar
For a thousand dancing words -

Revolve The Spinning Top

A speck of agitation is Self -
Moulded by atoms and deformed
By abstract hope -
Stillness?
Can it be gathered
Does its harvest yield, nourish
The discontent of argument?
Thoughts nearly always
Remain young even as the
Withered lips smile
The thoughtful idea is beauty - not age.

Being part of the spinning top
Myself and other selves
Are giddy with a sickness cast from space
That speeds hours born of clocks
As life is born when Time beckons -
Not the philosophers's time, that may or may not exist
Or the poet's time that dances and reclines
In tune to line or rhyme
Or the prisoner's time that marks off years
Slowly like a draught of poison from
A dank green bottle that doesn't kill,
When drunk destroys the soul
Just as the time of the damned is endless
Or the time of the blessed is restless even in paradise -

This space-time
This spinning top Time
Beckons and then quickens
And then grows like children
Too fast for the strength
Ever to regain its first health -
No Galileo is needed
To declare this star valid
The spinning top is its own
Windmill -
Just as myself makes claim
Only to pains felt -
Giving a sympathy for yours,
This star is master and mistress
Of the universe because nothing else
Has yet bettered it -

A mere spin-off from a too hot sun
A spinning globe of mystery
Probably doomed sooner or later -
The atoms seek revenge,
Either with great bangs and mushrooms
Made of fire or by a coldness called
The end -

Victory, brilliant and displayed like
The triumph of a battle shines
From the stars -
Follow us spinning top -
We have raged the black nothingness
Of light years dark without peace
To shine and sparkle and tempt
To glitter -
Yet we are dull - even dead -
Leaden dreams to your beautiful face -
All human matter contains in fragment
A piece of star-life - all selves
Joined together forever by objects
Still in their essence clinging to space -
Monopolised by a hazardous beginning
Making each self an island difficult
To reach, formed from a distant star
Whose energy is finished but whose
Venture within us continues to breathe -

Rimbaud's 'black and white moons'
Float and drift like balloons -
Until pricked by rays that scatter their
Pieces hither and thither through space-time
Where they shine everlasting pictures -
The spinning top holds star-history
Within rocks, within patterns of tree-wood
Within humanity's dreams of heaven -
Moving outwards, onward with
Terrible storms -
Yet always still within itself -
The known spinning top
Gathers speed - going where?
Whilst seas reflect space moods
As skies strike thunder at blue waves
And space-caves become filled with

A strange yet silent promise -

Were there perhaps foul stars
With gases evil, a core of badness
Swirling amid storms so terrible
That no imagination can touch their might
Only a grim mythology of giants, star-gods
And blood rimmed eyes can paint the
Sunrise of a diseased beginning -
And gentle perfect stars - perhaps
Falling, ever falling from a healthy sun
Which shines silver behind the moon's back
And laughing like pretty children laugh
At play as the spinning top experienced day
Then night - onward in space -
Yet seeming still -
The moving clouds, the rain showers -
And somewhere the desert sand -
So quick to tempest - so hard to understand -
Ever forward accurately passing
The shadowy black-holes which suck
All heaven's waste in
One absurd mouthful -
Into everlasting darkness -

Applied logic or controlled madness -
Even perhaps a feeble joke -
The spinning top gives its clues with care
The initiate's books tell of their theories -
Of dark beginnings, of matter going this way
Or that, of great lumps falling, joining,
Breaking up - of it all being strung together
Like balls of string.
Or chaos.
Forever.
Freezing, dark -

Poem Of Actuality

Today the sun shone -
It shone from early dawn -
Till well into evening -
To begin the day
I got up early
And was irritable -

After a bath
In warm water
I felt less irritable -
And relaxed with
My lover who was
More awake than me -

My son went to school
After eating a soft-boiled egg
My daughter went to London
With my sister
And a chap from a pop-group
Who also drove the mini -

I hoovered the rooms
Put the pyjamas away
While my lover read
The front page of the Daily Express
Quietly cursing himself
Quietly cursing me -

Really he loves me
And I love him
But our lives
Went rotten on us
Years ago
And we are struggling

To free our overburdened
Hearts and release our
Feet, so that we can run
Over the fields thro'
The long grass into
Our own oblivion -

But before we can do that -
I had to go and get some money

And my lover had to find
A car-park for the motor-bike -
Then we went to the market,
Buying salads and too much

Soft-fruit and tooth-picks,
Tissues and ribbon to type
This poem of actuality -
My lover drank hot -soup
And I drank weak tea
Waiting for the apple-crumble with cream -

Once he kissed the tip
Of my tanned nose and I
Stroked his hair -
When we returned to
The semi-furnished flat
Before he tiled the bathroom

He made love to me
And after supper in the
Warm July air he cleaned the 'bike
Said we were going to France -
And ate two cherries
From my hand -

Soon it will be bedtime -
And we'll make love again -
Because we are like that.
And really we love one another
But we'll fall asleep pretending
Its a 'summer-affair' -

And in the morning -
I'll be irritable again,
Because I hate getting-up early -

By the way I forgot to say
My lovers's name
Is Anthony -

Wasted Time

Yes, I've laid waste my time on useless men
Driven my passion on against my true identity -
Lost moments to boredom instead of to my pen
Been subject to the whim of my sexuality -
Found bitter essence there and nearly death -
Of brain, of truth, of self, being vexed and angry
With all my affairs and marriages, my lover's breath
Breaths on me only discontent. So find me
Now in the region of virtue near moral strength
Near nature's landscape, by the faithful sea -
Alone with gull or leaf, where at length
I can ride my daydream - turn my golden key

    To open a castle door, where love is divine -
    Cleansed and pure, sweet and mine all mine -

❖

Sunflowers

So Vincent you were consumed by sunflowers -
Nothing in the red-poppy fields assuaged
Your madness only made it worse -

You were caught, held between a violent sunset
And the twisted smile of an alley-whore.
You loved humanity for it suffered
But you loathed people and their lies -

For you the butterfly or snail
Dipped their existence into your paints
Touched your loneliness, dried your tears -

Ah! Vincent, the artist bleeds.
Poets die before believed -
Your pictures were but post-cards
Saying, 'Wish you were here' to a host
Of cold creatures who never see
The sunflower as a temple
Or the poppy as a god -

You found the torment and knew
That at the tip of your paint-brush
You held the world hostage -

Your madness was art being difficult
Your hurt now hangs on walls
Instead of in your heart -

Be still your sorrow -
Pictures are your yellow-fields
And silent ransom the price we pay
For your bullet wound -

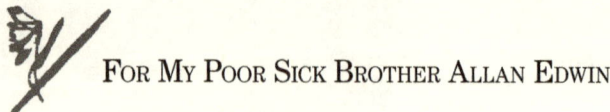

For My Poor Sick Brother Allan Edwin

I have not seen an angel
Or heard an holy voice -
Or witnessed a miracle -
Nor seen a saint -

But I have felt a peace -
A tenderness -
A token-wind of faith -

I have known a place -
Where a spirit played
Deep on my heart -
Played in my brain -

A touch of joy sped me along -
A path leading upward to His Cross -
And on my knees or standing
Near his church - I have felt
The nearness of a truth -
Conflict is banished into ash -
And high above reason, time or year
His precious call repeats
The message of a world to come -
'My people hear, oh! Hear'

Poet Follow Your Sadness

Poet follow your sadness
To the banks where willows weep -
Come Poet with your care
To the edge of moving waters
Steep with reeds -

Rest from deep emotion -
Poet of tangled hair -
See the swaying, crying willow
Shall weep for you -
Fair winds shall play tunes
Of summer on your face -

Move dear Poet of sorrow
Towards the flowing lake -
Take wings from ladybirds and flee
The hours of pain - rise above
All bitter knowledge and weave
A leaf or two of willow's hair -
Come Poet take hold of flowers
And smell the scent -

Be quick Poet, skilled with many voices
From the bottom of the lake
Find a magic stone - float it for your own -
Drink such waters almost holy
To refresh your hour of grace -
Back Poet to the time of words -
A creature whirled into fiery winds -
Spoken or cried, shouted or prayed -
You Poet are shaped to be scattered -

Be safe Poet -
Evil and good bend and break -
Across the willows' wet branches -
Clean tears towards a better Eden -
Gently wash your hands Poet
For a supper of willow-leaves -
Beneath trees the furious winds are quiet -
Now Poet see the land is glad
The pilgrim that you are is free

Eagles

Wild was the day
Wilder still the night -
Bright was the sun
Brighter still the stars -

Wild was our love
Still wilder our despair -
Wilder still our words
Birds that we were
Eagles both of us,
Wild on the wing
Wilder still our flight,
Thro' the wild days -
Flying into nights -

Bright was our love
Brighter still our tears -

Siste Viator

Stop Traveller -
Boredom evaporates desire
Even as fire burns itself to ash -
Your feet will touch and stay no longer -
Losing interest in maps and charts -
Peoples and their towns of historic value
Will nudge your boredom and at daybreak
You will take a look at castles plus churches
Then hurry to get some lunch with
Aching eyes from too much sun -
An irreparable damage to your heart
Makes you depart from all your longings -
Nothing holds the virtue that you've lost
And travelling become the countenance
Of lost truth -
Too many cities, too many days from Persia
To Peru, across to Samoa or Siam, through
Uruguay or Tunis, Romania and Venezuela,
Yugoslavia and all the lonely way back -
With postcards of Sarawak -
Words blow like a flag in your mind
   Vestigia nulla retrorsum
You have left nothing behind -
Taken nothing away -
You will not return this or any day
For your footsteps left no traces
Backward or forward you remain
Only bored
A strange peace mocks the empty suitcase -
The day the traveller stops

November Winds

(1)
    Bright red balloons
        Are my tears
    They blew away
        With a heavy breeze
    Also a beach ball
        That was blue
    And my youth that was white
        Blew away

(2)
    Pairs of shoes
        Skirts and tops
    Dresses of gold
        Blew away
    Music for dancing
        A pound of sweet-cherries
    And my father
        Blew away

(3)
    Laughter with friends
        Dinner plates
    With cold chops
        Blew into fragments
    Drums beat a dead song
        Little dogs, kittens and a yellow bird
    Blew into dust

(4)
    A dark haired child
        Once mine grew-up
    And was immediately
        Blown away -
    All my loves blown
        With every wish
    Across a patch of winter

(5)
    Tube trains caught
        With a dozen books
    White 'mac and old suits
        Green-shirts, a yellow scarf -
    Blown away, blown away, blown away

(6)
  A favourite house
  Field and three cows
  New lambs, green buses
  Leaf upon leaf
  Wild strawberries and a snow-storm
    Blown away -

(7)
  A long river
  Near some steps
  Paris in a day
  Swans, deer, hills and cars
  Shops in a glass of barley-wine -
  All mine - all blown away

(8)
  An Indian monsoon
  Raindrops for gods
  Songs out of flutes
  Sandals and rice on a fingertip -
  Blown away

(9)
  Blown away promise
  Blown away despair
  Blown away soul music
  Blown away hair - and fried chicken
  Blown away tickets for
  'Alls Well, That Ends Well'
  Blown, blown, blown
  All my bulbs for next year's
    Spring flowers

❖

On The Steps Of Morning

On the steps of morning
The clock struck -
One, two, three
A blackbird sang,
With a wren for company -
A hawk-moth with the stillness
Of stone lay undisturbed,
On the horizon specks
Of what appeared to be lovers
Twisted themselves into the hour.
With the fastidiousness of unmarried aunts,
Wildness of startled beasts became calm -
Never tame!

Time held between two fingers
Quickened the hour.
If a conjurer had called,
'Vanish'
The unreasonable request
Would be ignored -
The conjurer wedged
Into a slice of rock.
The clock struck
Four, five, six -
Farewell pick-up-sticks -
Anxious voices dissembled
From joy, apologise to
Nothing -
A weak halo of sunlight changed
Morning to afternoon.

What nonsense is revealed
Listening to sea-shells -
Elaborate stories wrung
From stale legends -
Placid photographs taken
Mistaken for charm - a pretending -
Seven, eight, nine -
A surge of lessons
Learnt, hated, forgotten -
Confidences shattered
Broken with faint care -
Abandoned by a wayside bridge -
The tired kitten, the withered rose -

Twilight reveals odd shapes -
Floating stars litter the sky
A particular craving enters
The hour - a craving not to be
Condemned -

On the steps of night
The clock strikes
Ten, eleven, twelve -
Dark is the escaping minute -
The companion of gloom is
Imagination -
Disillusioned with predictions -
The owl watches -
The bat flies -
Mediocre dreams pour into sleepers unaware
Of marvellous moonlight
Playing on window-panes -
Waiting to flower, anemones
Lie in damp earth -
As the blackbird's egg is blue
And pale is the jonquil's petal -
Morning will come -

www.ingramcontent.com/pod-product-compliance
Lightning Source LLC
Chambersburg PA
CBHW051720040426
42446CB00008B/974